Art & Activities for Kids

Make Gifts!

Kim Solga

Cincinnati, Ohio

Note to Parents and Teachers

The activities in this book were developed for the enjoyment of children. We've taken every precaution to ensure their safety and success. Please follow the directions, and note where an adult's help is required. In fact, feel free to work alongside your young artists as often as you can. They will appreciate help in reading and learning new techniques, and will love the chance to talk and show off their creations. Children thrive on attention and praise, and art adventures are the perfect setting for both.

Make Gifts! Copyright © 1991 by F&W Publications, Inc. Printed and bound in Hong Kong. All rights reserved. No part of this book may be reproduced in any form or by any electronic or mechanical means including information storage and retrieval systems without permission in writing from the publisher, except by a reviewer, who may quote brief passages in a review. Published by North Light Books, an imprint of F&W Publications, Inc., 1507 Dana Avenue, Cincinnati, Ohio 45207. First edition.

95 94 93 92   5 4 3 2

Library of Congress Cataloging in Publication Data

Solga, Kim.
  Make Gifts! / Kim Solga. — 1st ed.
      p.   cm.
  Summary: Readers learn how to make a variety of craft gifts including jewelry, sculpture, cards, calendars, containers, wrapping paper, and more.
  ISBN 0-89134-386-5
  1. Handicraft — Juvenile literature.   2. Gifts — Juvenile literature.
  [1. Handicraft. — 2. Gifts.]   I. Title.
TT160.S59 1991
745.5 — dc20   91-2502
                                                                   CIP
                                                                    AC

Edited by Julie Wesling Whaley
Designed by Clare Finney
Photography Direction by Kristi Kane Cullen
Art Production by Suzanne Whitaker
Photography by Pamela Monfort
Very special thanks to Mandy Garcia, Max Magac, Lara Muehlenbach and Niki Smith.

Make Gifts! features eleven unique projects that will fire the imagination of boys and girls ages six to eleven and will result in quality presents kids will be proud to give. By inviting children to design their own gifts, *Make Gifts!* encourages individual creativity. Young artists will love doing these activities even while they're learning the importance of fine craftsmanship. And they'll be learning composition and design, working with color and texture, and planning symmetry versus abstract design.

Make Gifts! involves not only artistic skills, but also fine motor skills and problem solving. Kids will engineer pop-up cards and plan functional calendars. They'll get a workout pounding hardware into wood. They'll create gift bundles that smell good. They'll gain experience in many different craft media. Giving crafted gifts satisfies kids' need for recognition of their work, something not achievable with store-bought gifts. All the projects are kid-tested to ensure success and inspire confidence.

Collecting Supplies

All of the projects can be done with household items or inexpensive, easy-to-find supplies. Here are some household items you'll want to make sure you have on hand: empty cans, bottles and jars; scrap paper and scrap cloth; sponges; metal pieces and hardware; newspapers; paper plates; masking tape and duct tape; string, ribbon and yarn; foam trays; sandpaper; paper towels; a muffin tin; an old toothbrush.

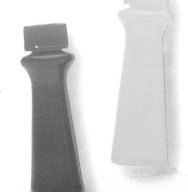

Be a Good Artist

Get permission to work at your chosen workspace before you begin. Cover your workspace with newspapers or a vinyl tablecloth.

Wear a smock or big, old shirt to protect your clothes.

Follow the directions carefully for each project. When you see the adult and child symbol, have an adult help you.

Don't put art materials in your mouth, and if you're working with a younger child, don't let him put art materials in his mouth, either.

The clock symbol means you must wait to let something dry before going on to the next step. It is very important not to rush ahead.

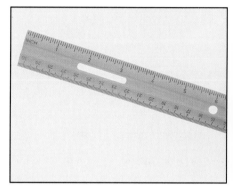

This symbol, ″, means inches—12″ means 12 inches; cm means centimeters. This symbol, ′, means feet—8′ means 8 feet; m means meters.

Some of the projects will require materials you will have to buy. Just remember that the money you spend on supplies is part of your special gift.

If you are careless, you might hurt yourself while you're building. Have fun, but be careful and treat all your tools with respect.

Always finish by cleaning your workspace and all of your tools.

Art Materials

Carpenter's glue. A special glue for wood sold at the hardware store. It's stronger than regular white glue. It's water soluble and nontoxic.

Crepe paper. Thin, colored streamers sold at dime stores in rolls. Crepe paper is commonly used to decorate for birthday parties.

Embroidery floss. Colored cotton thread sold at needlework stores and craft stores. It comes in skeins.

Tempera paint. A water-based paint that is opaque—you can't see through it. You can buy it in an art supply store already mixed with water (a liquid paint in a bottle or jar) or as a powder that you can mix yourself.

Watercolor paint. A water-based paint that is transparent—you can see through it when you paint with it. It comes in little trays of dry paint that you wet with a paintbrush and water.

Acrylic paint. A water-based plastic paint that's thick and shiny. It comes in a tube or squeeze bottle. You mix it with water to paint, but it's permanent once it's dry.

Paintbrushes. There are many kinds of brushes for different uses. You may want to buy several, from fine-point watercolor brushes to square, heavy-bristle brushes. It's fun to paint with big brushes from the hardware store, too!

Varnish. Acrylic gloss medium is a nontoxic varnish sold at art supply stores. Regular varnish, like shellac, has toxic fumes and requires paint thinner to clean up, so *always* get an adult to help you if you use regular varnish. Clear nail polish makes a good varnish, but get permission before you use it.

Trophies

Trophies are for winners, and anyone who gets one of these handmade awards is a winner for sure! Each trophy is a sculpture—a one-of-a-kind character you design yourself. It's fun to build trophies using materials related to whatever the award is. Here are instructions for making The World's Greatest Cook trophy. Look on pages 10-11 for more ideas—or make up your own!

Materials needed:

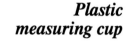

Plastic measuring cup

White glue

Macaroni

Scissors

Things to make a face

1 Glue macaroni onto the measuring cup head to make a wild hairdo. Work slowly, letting the glue dry as you work.

2 Draw a smiling face with a felt-tip pen, or glue on raisins or other small things a cook would use. Let this dry overnight.

3 Cover the empty can with construction paper. Carefully cut small slits into two sides. Stick the plastic spoons in for the arms.

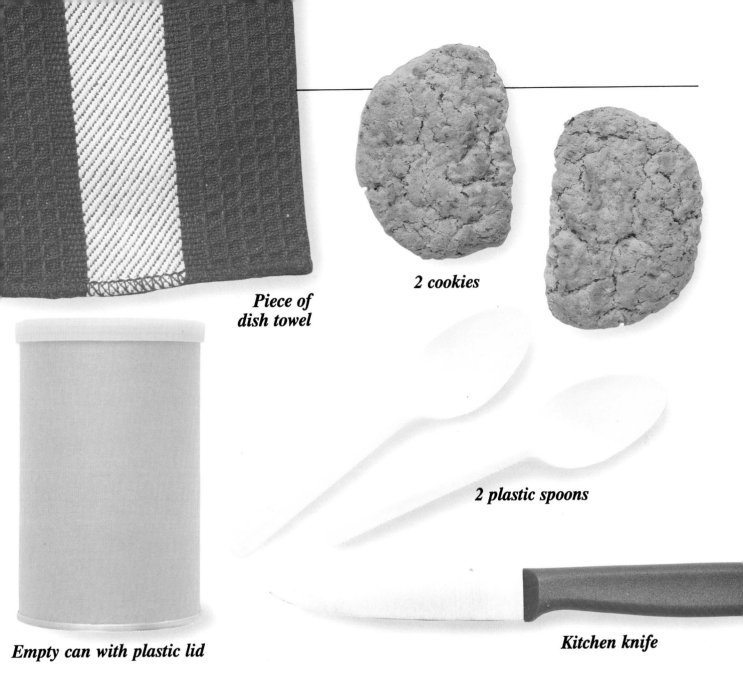

*Piece of
dish towel*

2 cookies

2 plastic spoons

Empty can with plastic lid

Kitchen knife

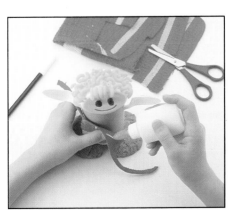

4 Glue the cookies onto the bottom of the can for big, sturdy feet. Cut a slit into the plastic lid and slip in the measuring cup head.

5 Cut a little apron out of the dish towel piece and glue it in place on the front of the body. Use construction paper if you don't have a spare towel.

6 Cut a banner out of construction paper. Use your best handwriting to print The World's Greatest Cook! Glue it to the front of the trophy.

The World's Greatest . . .

It's fun to invent other "World's Greatest" trophies. What could you use to make a trophy for a fisherman, a computer whiz, a football player, or your favorite babysitter?

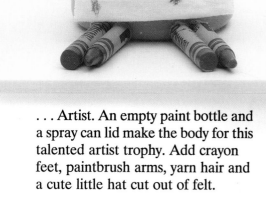

. . . Artist. An empty paint bottle and a spray can lid make the body for this talented artist trophy. Add crayon feet, paintbrush arms, yarn hair and a cute little hat cut out of felt.

. . . Cook. Who's the best cook in your family?

. . . Golfer. Do you know someone who likes to play golf? Ask if you can have an old golf club cover, some tees and ball markers, and a little score pencil. Then surprise him with his own Greatest Golfer trophy!

World's Greatest Teacher

WORLD'S GREATEST GOLFER

. . . Teacher. Give this to your teacher on the last day of school! Use a chalkboard eraser for the body, with pink eraser feet, yellow pencil arms, thumbtack eyes, and hair made from the spiral wire from an old notebook.

Handmade Paper

The paper we use every day is made in factories. But handmade paper is much more interesting and great fun to make in your own kitchen. **Get permission** to do this project, or get an adult to help you.

You will start by making *pulp*, a goopy mixture of paper fibers and water. Tear scraps of paper into tiny pieces and blend them with lots of water. You can even let the torn paper scraps soak in water overnight to make it easier on your blender. To make a really strong piece of paper, grind the pulp in the blender for 2 or 3 minutes until only the fibers are left.

Blender and water

Materials needed:

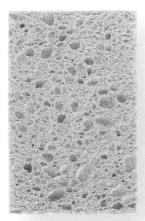

Sponge

Scraps of paper and cloths or towels

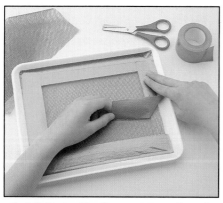

1 Make a dipping screen: Cut the center out of a clean foam meat tray. Cut a piece of window screen to fit the hole and tape it to the tray.

2 Tear stationery, computer paper, business cards, index cards, and envelopes into small pieces. Don't use newspaper, paper towels, or tissues.

3 Fill the blender ¾ full of water. Turn it on low and *slowly* add a handful of paper pieces. Use *lots* of water and not much paper, or you'll ruin the blender.

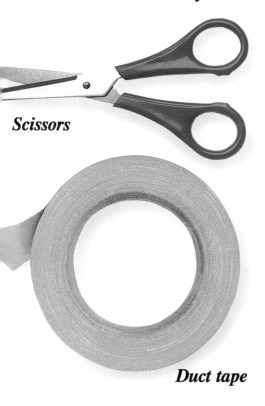

Plastic dishpan and a board

Piece of window screen
Foam meat tray

Scissors

Duct tape

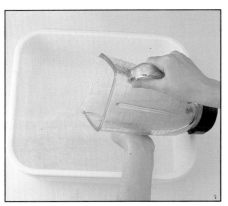

4 Grind the paper into a soupy mash (called pulp). Pour the water and pulp into the dishpan half full of water. The pulp will float! Do this 5 to 6 times.

5 Slip your dipping screen into the water under the floating pulp. Lift it straight up, catching a thin layer of pulp on the screen.

6 Gently flip the screen over onto a damp towel. Pat the back of the screen with a wet sponge to release the layer of pulp.

13

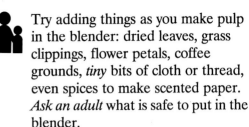
Try adding things as you make pulp in the blender: dried leaves, grass clippings, flower petals, coffee grounds, *tiny* bits of cloth or thread, even spices to make scented paper. *Ask an adult* what is safe to put in the blender.

7 Lift off the screen and fold the towel over on top of the pulp. Repeat this process until you have several layers of pulp between layers of towel or cloth.

8 Place the stack of towels and paper on the basement floor or outside on the sidewalk. Put the board on top and stand on it to squeeze out the water.

9 Peel back the towel and *very gently* work your fingers under the paper and lift it off. Do this for each piece of paper, and put them on a flat surface to dry overnight.

You can also decorate handmade
paper after you flip it off the screen
onto the towel. Pat any small, flat
object into it. Try dried flowers, strips
of ribbon, or tiny stars and sequins.
Then press the paper and let it dry.

15

Hardware Art

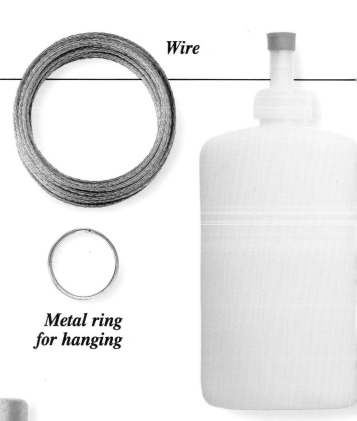

Wire

Metal ring for hanging

Carpenter's glue

These rugged sculptures look especially good outdoors in a garden or patio. Rain and sun add a special beauty as the years go by. Start with plain, soft wood like redwood or cedar, an interesting piece of weathered wood from an old fence or barn, or a pretty piece of flat driftwood.

Collect interesting old nails and metal tools: nails, screws, bolts, nuts, washers, horseshoe nails, furniture tacks, hinges, drawer pulls, bottle caps, wire, and springs. Ask a carpenter for old bits of hardware, look for small machine parts, or get permission to take an old clock apart for its gears and metal parts.

Be careful. *Work slowly* to avoid accidents, and *ask for help* if you need it.

Materials needed:

A piece of wood and hammer

Metal pieces, pencil and paper

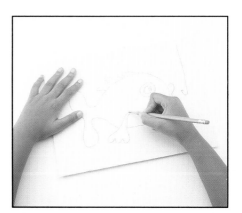

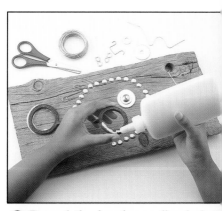

1 Design your picture on paper before you begin. Try drawing an animal—birds and fish are good—or a face or a giant sunflower.

2 Sketch your design onto the wood. Hammer rows of nails or tacks into the wood, following your outline. Fill in the shapes with other pieces of hardware.

3 Pound the hardware firmly into the board. Wire things onto staples to hold them in place, or use carpenter's glue to stick things in place.

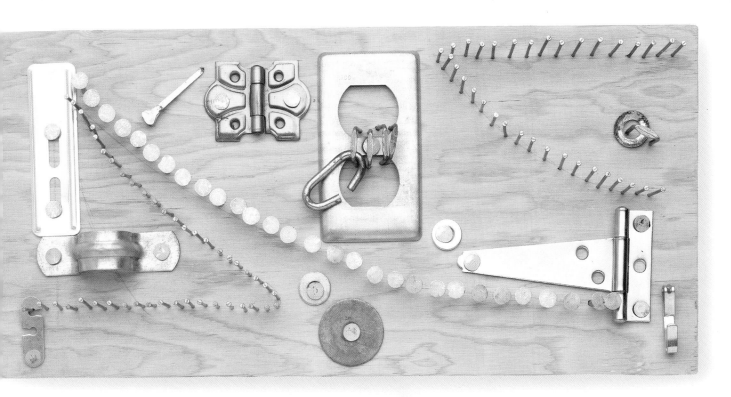

Abstract designs are fun to make. You can work from a sketch or just start hammering nails into the wood, making interesting patterns, and adding bits of hardware wherever you like. Attach a metal ring to the back or top of your finished sculpture so it can be hung like a picture.

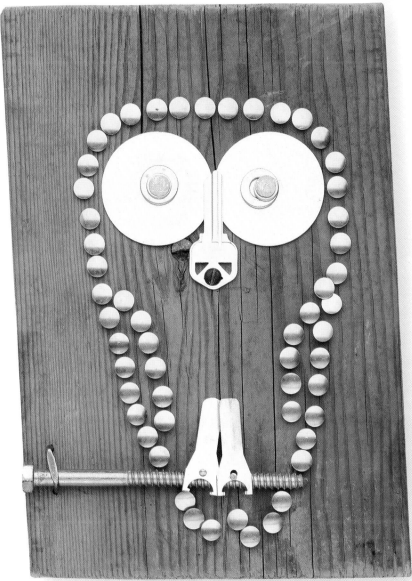

Hardware Owl

Special Scents

Make fragrant bundles for Mom, Dad, Grandma, even your pet dog or cat! Follow these recipes or create your own—let your nose be your guide. Whenever you use something that needs to be dried, like lemon or orange peel or flower petals, spread them out on a plate and set them in a warm, dark place for one week. Ideas for scented gifts you can make are on the next two pages.

Spicy mix
Peel an orange and cut the peels into small squares and dry them. Put a cinnamon stick into a sock and pound it into small chunks with a hammer. Mix equal parts of dried orange peel, cinnamon chunks and whole cloves.

Aromatic mix
Gather needles from a pine tree and dry them. Mix a handful of dry pine needles with several spoonfuls of dried herbs such as rosemary, oregano, bay leaves and thyme.

Flower mix
Gather flower petals, especially rose petals, and dry them. Dried petals smell great all by themselves, or you can sprinkle a few drops of perfume on them for even more fragrance.

Pet mix

Combine cedar chips (sold at pet supply stores) with drops of eucalyptus oil (sold at a pharmacy) for a nonchemical flea and bug repellant.

Mint mix

Gather fresh mint leaves and dry them, or use mint tea. Peel a lemon and cut the peels into small squares and dry them. Mix equal parts of dried lemon peel and mint.

Other smells

Combine any of these to create your own mixtures: scrapings from scented soaps and candles, dried lavender leaves and blossoms, herb teas, baby powder and bath crystals.

Scented Gifts

Sweet Hearts

Cut two heart shapes out of felt, each about as big as the palm of your hand. Spread a thin line of glue along the edge of one heart. Place a small amount of scented mix in the center of the heart and lay the second heart on top. Pinch the edges with your fingers until they stick together. Decorate the hearts with glued-on sequins, beads, glitter, lace and bows.

Sachet Bundles

Cut a 6″-square (15cm) or round piece of thin fabric (an old nylon stocking is perfect). Place a large spoonful of scented mix in the middle and pull the edges of the cloth up around it. Tie it with a ribbon or piece of yarn, and trim the top of the cloth to make a fluff above the tie.

Itty Bitty Bags

Cut a 4″ by 6″ (10 cm by 15 cm) piece of cloth. Have an adult help you stitch up three sides of the bag, inside out. Then turn it right side out, fill it with scented mix, and tie it closed with a piece of string or yarn. If you stuff them with pet mix, itty bitty bags become natural "mothballs."

Pet Pillow

Have an adult help you sew a cushion (like a bag but bigger, and easier to sew on a sewing machine). Make it big enough for your pet to sleep on, and stuff it with pet mix. Or have an adult help you stitch up a bandana and stuff it with pet mix for a natural flea collar.

Gifts for Men, Women and Babies

Make a small cushion for dad or grandpa by stuffing one of their old ties. Mom or grandma might like a little basket filled with scented mix. Make a bundle for a baby by stuffing a bootie with scented mix. Tie it closed with a pink or blue ribbon.

Seashell Boats

Fill little shells with scented mix. Wrap the whole shell with a piece of nylon stocking, lace or netting. Tie it with a ribbon and add tiny shell decorations.

Gift Calendars

What's your favorite holiday? Is it Valentine's Day or Christmas, the last day of school or your own birthday? You can celebrate them all, and even invent new holidays as you make this special calendar. It's a great gift for someone to use and enjoy all year.

Materials needed:

Glue or clear adhesive tape

Felt-tip pens

Pencil

1 Trace or draw the boxes for each day, one page for each month, using a printed calendar as a guide (many businesses give them away for free).

2 Write the names of the days of the week across the top of each month and number the boxes. Write neatly and follow the guide calendar carefully.

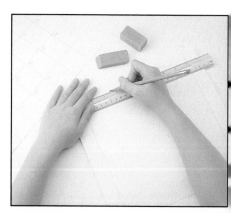

3 Make an art page for each month. Draw a frame around each art page about 1″ (3 cm) in from the sides.

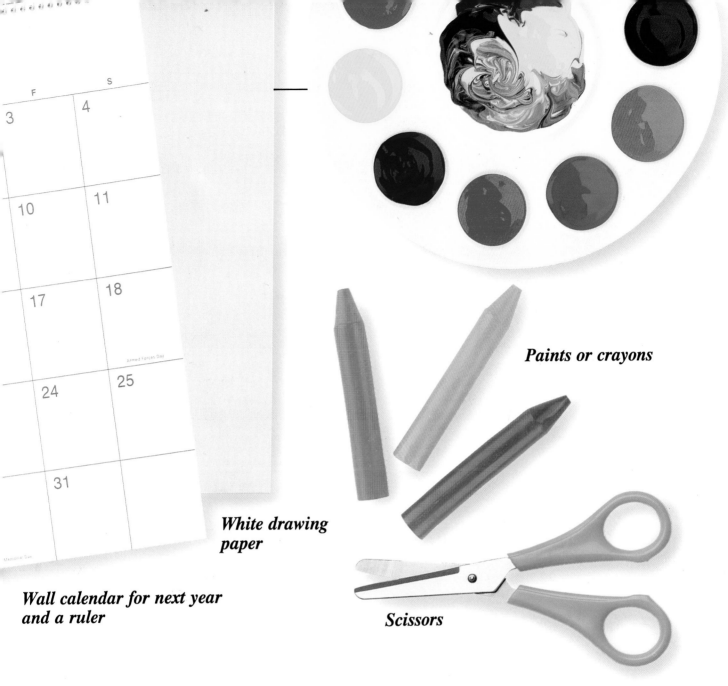

Paints or crayons

White drawing paper

Wall calendar for next year and a ruler

Scissors

4 Pick a holiday or special event and draw a picture for it—or draw a scene that celebrates the whole month.

5 Color each picture with bright crayons or paints. Draw small pictures or designs in the border and color them in, too.

6 Use a felt-tip pen to carefully go over all the words on your calendar. Use fancy lettering for a special look.

Art Pages for Calendars

Glue your pages onto the pages of a
ready-made calendar. Or, tie, glue, or
tape your pages to each other, using
the ready-made calendar as a guide.

Container Mania

These bright and beautiful containers make great gifts because they have so many uses. They can be pen and pencil holders, flower-pots, kitchen utensil holders — make lots of containers to hold anything you need to store. You can decorate a container and then fill it with little things for a really special present. Start with a glass or plastic bottle or jar or empty can with a smooth edge on top, and make sure it's clean and dry.

Paper plate

Materials needed:

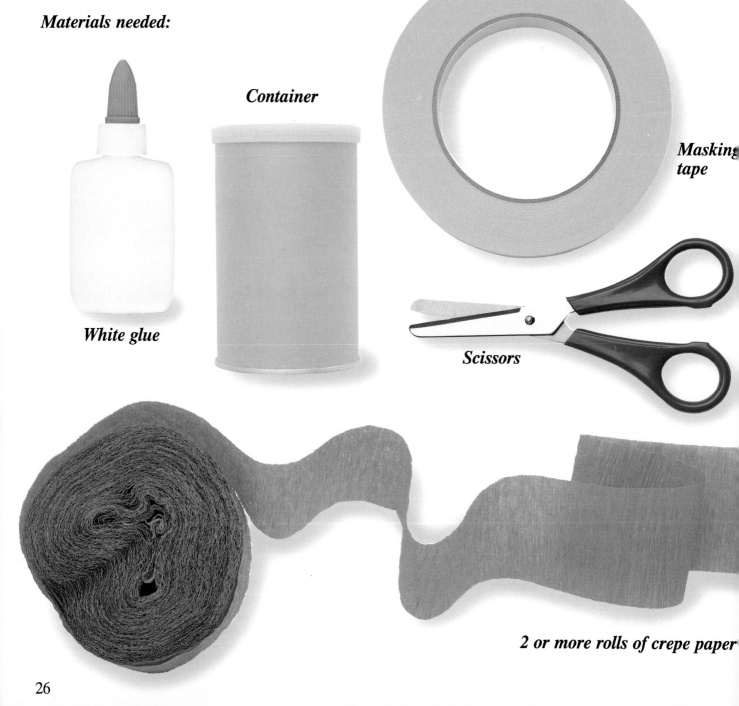

White glue

Container

Masking tape

Scissors

2 or more rolls of crepe paper

Water and bowl for mixing

Paintbrush

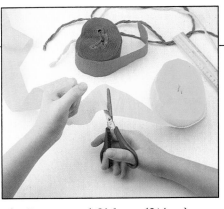

1 Cut several 8'-long (2½ m) strips of crepe paper. Twist them as tight as you can until they look like a rope.

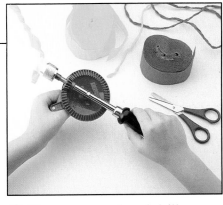

2 You can use a hand drill or egg beater to help twist. Tape one end of the crepe paper to the drill bit or beater and have someone hold the other end while you crank.

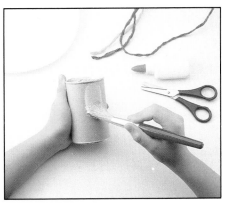

3 Squirt some glue onto the paper plate and use the paintbrush to smear a 1″ (3 cm) strip of glue up the side of the container.

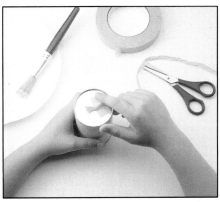

4 Tape one end of the crepe paper rope to the bottom of the container. Wrap the rope around the container, pressing it into the layer of glue.

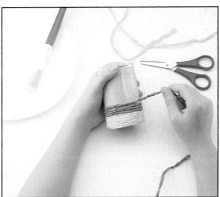

5 Push the rows of rope close together. Spread more glue if you need it. When you use up one piece of rope, cut the end, stick it into the glue, and start another.

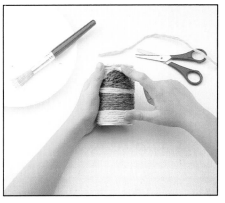

6 Wrap the paper rope up to the top and cut it and glue it down. If you want to use a cover on your container, leave a little space at the top so it will fit.

Crafty Containers

▼ Let the paper rope dry for an hour. Then mix equal parts of glue and water and brush the mixture over the top of the paper to protect it.

 ▶ Tear off little strips of masking tape and cover a bottle by overlapping the pieces. Go over i with black or brown shoe polish fc a leathery look.

▼ Wrap a can with a cloth or plastic measuring tape to make a sewing kit. Glue a tomato pincushion onto the plastic lid and add a few stick pins. Fill it with a pack of needles and several spools of thread for a handy gift anyone can use.

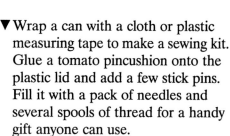

▲ Twist colorful or shiny gift wrap ribbon with the crepe paper, or add fuzzy mohair yarn or bumpy chenille yarn for a different look.

▼ Glue crayons in a row around a small can to make a colorful pencil holder. Or glue a crazy collection of stuff to make a special "junk" container of your own design.

◄ Wrap a container with rope and add a bob or lure or some other finishing touch. Fill it with things your favorite fisherman will need on his next outing.

String Pictures

Geometry is the secret behind these elegant wall hangings. They look so professional, no one will believe you made them yourself! Start with fiberboard, cork, or foam-core board and cover it with felt or colored paper. Hang your finished string art by attaching a pop-top from a soda can to the back with a thumbtack.

Materials needed:

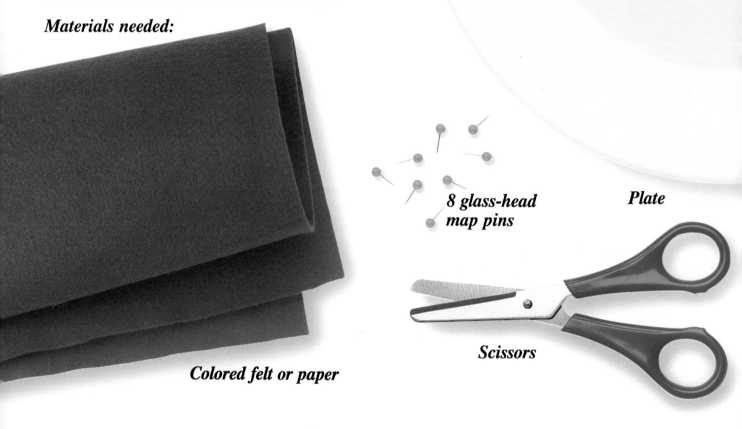

8 glass-head map pins

Plate

Scissors

Colored felt or paper

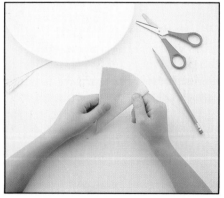

1 Trace a dinner plate on a piece of paper and cut out the circle. Fold it in half, then in half again (into fourths), then again (into pie-slice shaped eighths).

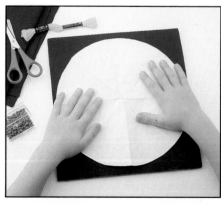

2 Unfold the circle and place it in the center of your covered board with one fold going straight up and down. Imagine the folds are numbered 1 through 8, with 1 at the top.

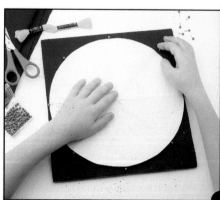

3 Stick a pin into the board at the end of every fold, right next to the paper circle. Leave the pins sticking up a little. When all 8 pins are in place, remove the paper.

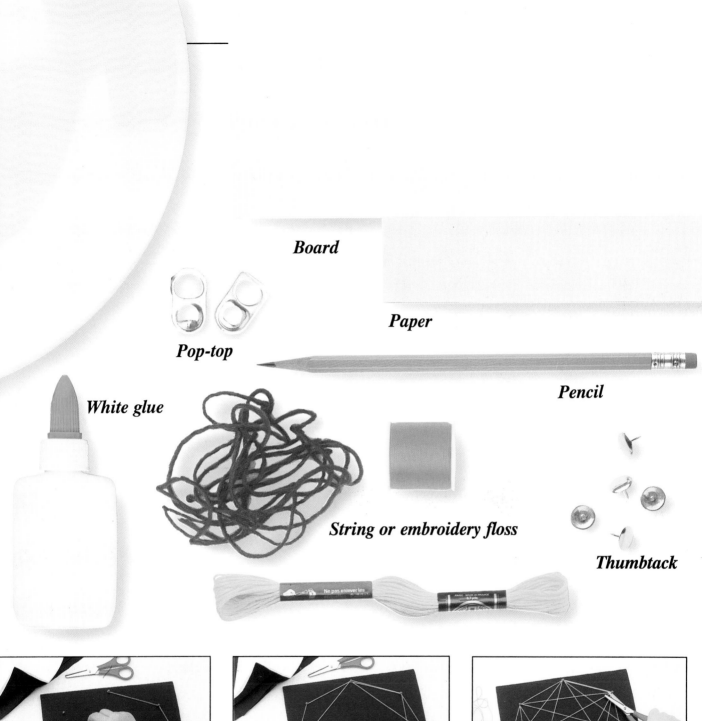

Board

Paper

Pop-top

Pencil

White glue

String or embroidery floss

Thumbtack

4 Tie one end of the string onto pin number 1 and begin winding around the circle. Go from 1 to 2, 2 to 3, and so on, making a loop (but not a knot) around each pin.

5 Keep the string tight (but don't pull the pins loose). After you've looped around the circle, go around it again in this order: 1 3 5 7 1 2 4 6 8.

6 Now go around the circle one last time, looping the pins in this order: 2 5 8 3 6 1 4 7 2. Make a knot when you get back to 2 and cut the string.

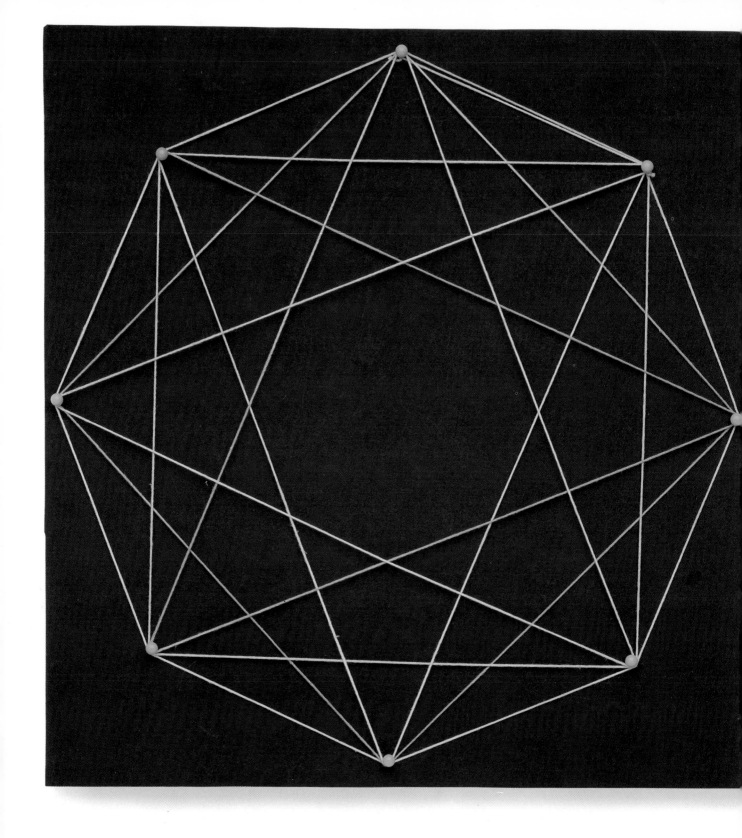

Try making a design using sewing thread—it's very delicate! Multicolored string and metallic thread look great, too.

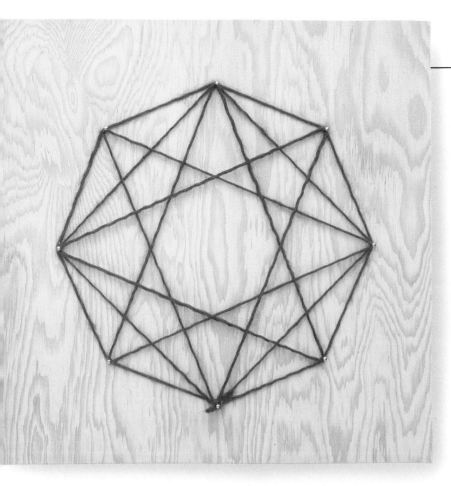

Try using different kinds of string. Yarn and twine look best in big designs. They're heavy, so use nails instead of pins.

Once you've mastered an 8-point circle, try a 16-point circle design! Fold the paper circle in half four times into skinny, pie-slice shaped sixteenths. Then follow the same steps, looping string around every pin, then every other pin, then every third pin, then every fourth pin, and so on.

Name Sculptures

Turn anyone's name into a special present with clay or dough. Make your own salt clay (that you let air dry to harden) or baker's dough (that you bake in the oven). Or use different colors of ready-made dough you can buy at toy stores, and let it air dry to harden.

Materials needed:

Salt clay

Mix 1½ cups of white flour, 1½ cups salt, 1 tablespoon of oil and enough water to make a smooth, soft clay (about ½ cup). Store in plastic in the refrigerator. Salt clay will dry hard if you leave it out overnight.

Nameplate Wall Hanging

1 Design the nameplate on paper before you begin. Make a full-size drawing so you'll know how big to make the dough plaque.

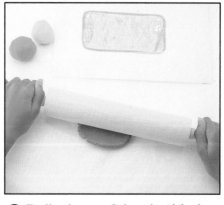

2 Roll a lump of dough with the rolling pin until it's ¼″ (⅔cm) thick. Cut off the edges to make a rectangle.

3 Roll dough in your hands to make long snakes. Make a frame and the letters you need and press them onto the nameplate.

Baker's dough

Mix 4 cups of white flour with 1 cup salt. Stir well, then add about 1½ cups of warm water. Knead until the dough is smooth. Have an adult help you bake the things you make with bakers dough in a 300°F oven until they're golden brown. **Don't try to eat** your bread creations—they're for decoration only.

Acrylic paint

Paintbrush, pencils, and paper

Varnish (optional)

Knife and spoon

Yarn, string or ribbon, and felt

Rolling pin (and waxed paper)

4 Add decorations made out of dough: flowers and leaves, sports equipment, a teddy bear, or simple balls or heart shapes.

5 Poke two holes in the top corners of the rectangle with the bottom of a pencil.

6 Dry or bake the nameplate according to the recipe. Tie yarn, string or ribbon through the holes.

You can knead food coloring into salt clay before sculpting your nameplate if you wish. Or you can paint the clay after it dries.

This desk plaque was made out of baker's dough brushed with egg yolk before baking to make it golden.

Desk Plaque

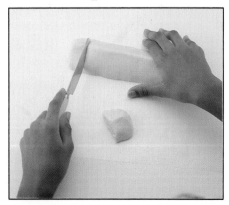

1 Roll a fat log of dough in your hands. Pinch and flatten it into a triangle shape. Trim the edges straight up and down.

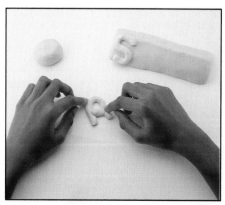

2 Roll snakes to form letters and press them onto one side of the triangle. Add decorations to the front and back sides.

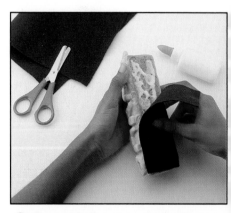

3 Dry or bake your desk plaque. Paint and varnish it if you wish. Glue a piece of soft cloth or felt on the bottom.

You can make other gifts with your clay or dough, such as ornaments, beads, and jewelry.

 You may want to have an adult help you brush a coat of clear varnish on your finished sculpture after it dries. It will protect it and make it shiny.

Free-Standing Sculptures

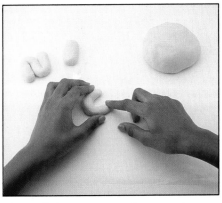

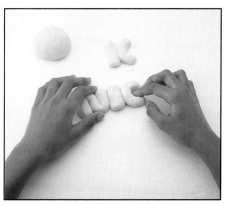

1 Roll fat sausage shapes of dough with your hands. Bend and mold them into big, puffy letters.

2 Gently press these fat letters together to make a name that stands by itself, either up and down or across.

3 Bake or dry your sculpture. Paint each letter a different color, with stripes and polka dots.

Pop Jewelry

Save the sticks from frozen pops or buy a bag of craft sticks at a hobby or art supply store. Use them to make pins, necklaces and keychains decorated like all kinds of animals.

Materials needed:

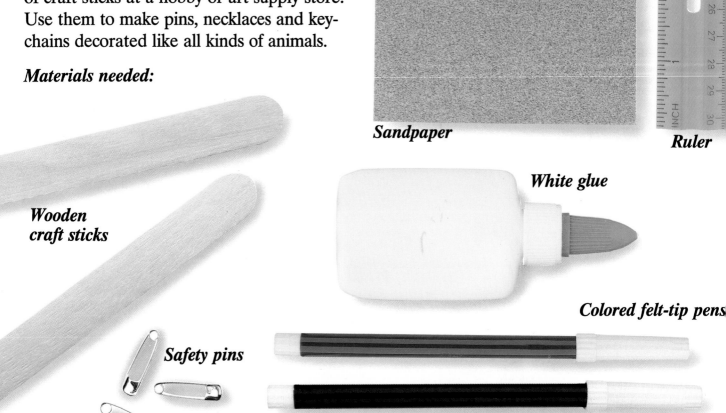

Sandpaper

Ruler

White glue

Colored felt-tip pens

Wooden craft sticks

Safety pins

Pencil

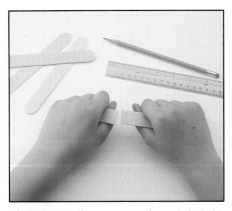

1 Draw a line across the stick 1½″ (4 cm) from the end. Scrape your fingernail along this line to make a groove. Bend and break the stick along the groove.

2 Rub the broken end with sandpaper until it's very smooth. Draw an animal design onto the wood with pencil, then color it in with bright felt-tip pens.

3 To make a pin, attach a safety pin to the back with a line of white glue. Hold the pin up out of the glue until it sets. Then let it dry overnight.

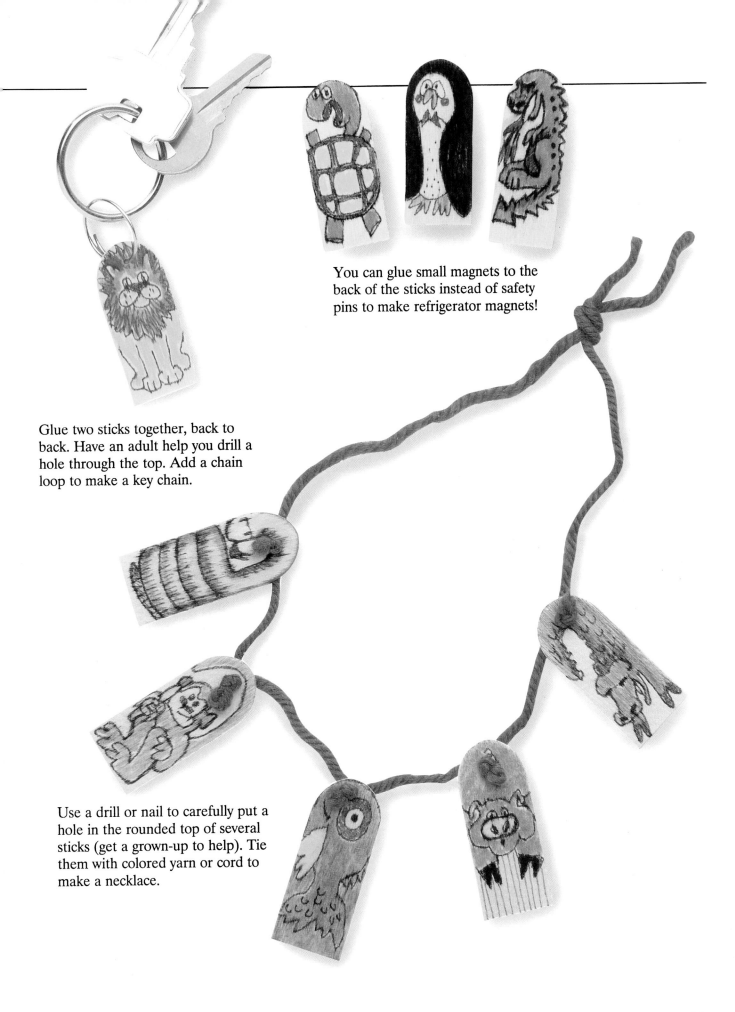

You can glue small magnets to the back of the sticks instead of safety pins to make refrigerator magnets!

Glue two sticks together, back to back. Have an adult help you drill a hole through the top. Add a chain loop to make a key chain.

Use a drill or nail to carefully put a hole in the rounded top of several sticks (get a grown-up to help). Tie them with colored yarn or cord to make a necklace.

Happy Wrapping

Get wrapped up in the fun of giving presents with wonderful gift wrap you make yourself. For a really special touch, make gift cards to match!

Materials needed:

Watercolors or tempera paint

White paper towels

Food coloring

Rainbow Wrap

1 For each color you want to use, mix 12 or more drops of food coloring with ¼ cup of water in muffin tins. Create your own colors!

2 Fold paper towels into squares and odd shapes. Dip the corners and edges into different colors — just enough to absorb some color without getting soaked.

3 Gently unfold the wet paper towel. Hang it on a clothesline or spread it flat on plastic or waxed paper to dry.

*Muffin tin, a spoon,
and water*

*Old toothbrush and a
cardboard box*

*A variety of papers, ribbon,
and yarn*

Paintbrushes

Natural Beauties

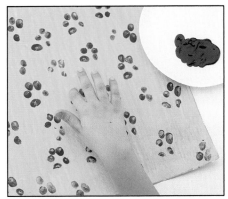

Zebra Wrap. Paint 1″ (3 cm) black stripes across white paper. Use a photo of a zebra as a guide — the stripes get thick and then thin, and some stripes blend together.

Leopard Wrap. Paint a piece of paper light gold and let it dry. Then dip your fingers into a shallow dish of black paint. Make patterns of dots all over the paper with your fingers.

Moo Wrap. Big black patches on white paper look like the side of a Holstein cow. Tie this package with grass-green ribbon and add a tiny cow bell cut from an egg carton.

Wrap It Up

Moo Wrap

Crumple Wrap

Crumple Wrap

1 Crumple a sheet of newspaper into a ball and dip it into a shallow dish of paint.

2 Pat the newspaper all over a piece of construction paper. The wrinkled paper creates a beautiful crackle pattern.

3 When your newspaper gets too soggy, throw it away and crumple up a fresh piece.

Rainbow Wrap

Star Wrap

Star Wrap

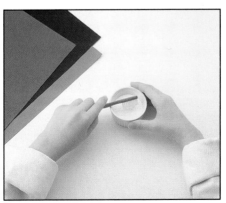

1 Lay a piece of dark construction paper in the bottom of a big cardboard box.

2 Dip the tip of an old toothbrush into white tempera paint. Hold the toothbrush in the box.

3 Rub your thumb across the bristles, splattering tiny dots of white paint onto the paper. Soon it will look like a starry sky.

Pop-Up Cards

Glue

Do you have paper, scissors and glue? Then you'll never need to buy another greeting card! Make your own birthday and holiday cards with these crazy pop-up critters. Put a special message inside the mouth for a great surprise. Look on pages 47-48 for other fun and easy cards to make.

Scissors

Materials needed:

Crayons

Plastic eyes, feathers, string and decorations

Frog Card

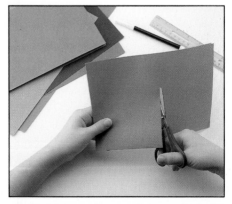

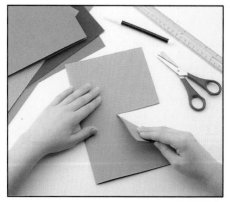

1 Fold two pieces of paper in half. One will be the card cover. Cut a slit across the other paper, from the middle of the fold to 2″ (6 cm) from the edges.

2 Fold the paper (on the bottom side of the cut) down to make a triangle. Fold it all the way out to the end of the cut.

3 Fold the paper (on the top side of the cut) up to make another triangle. This fold should be ½″ (1½ cm) in from the end of the cut.

**Construction paper
(9" by 12" or size A4)**

Felt-tip pens and a ruler

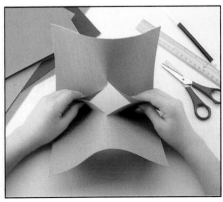

4 Open the paper flat and gently pull the triangle sections so they both fold toward you. Fold the paper in half again, this time with both triangles tucked to the inside.

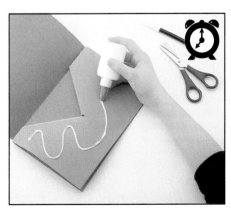

5 Spread glue on the parts of the paper that show. Wrap the cover around the outside. Press and wait a few minutes for the glue to set.

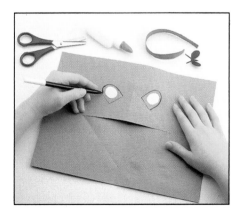

6 When you open your card, the triangle sections pull together to make a big mouth! Draw a face or use paper scraps or decorations to finish your card.

Make a green frog with a tongue that really dangles out the mouth. Add a fly for the frog to aim for!

Create a fierce fish with scissor teeth that just fit together as he opens and shuts his mouth.

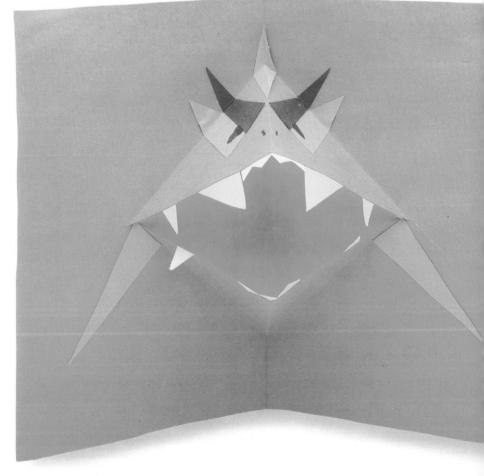

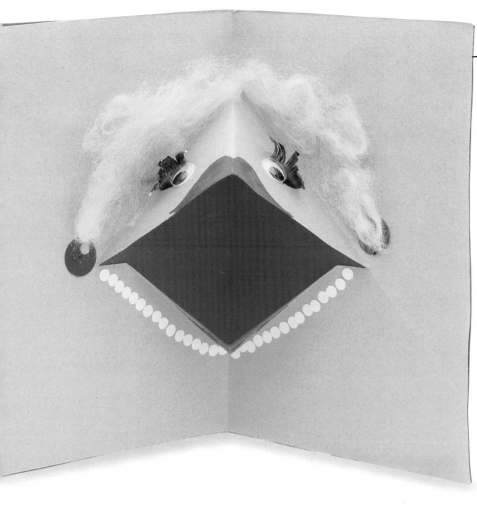

Make a person with wiggly eyes and string for hair. Or make a bird and use feathers to decorate.

Build a different kind of peek-a-boo card by drawing a house or castle with lots of windows and doors. Cut around them so they'll fold open and shut. Glue this picture onto another paper, being careful not to glue the windows down. Open them and draw faces or messages.

Other Greeting Cards

You're the Star
Make a photocopy of a photo of the person you want to make a card for. Cut out the face and glue it onto a folded paper. Draw and color a picture around it. Turn people into TV stars, sports heroes, clowns— anything!

Nature's Cards
Collect small leaves and flowers. Lay them gently between pieces of paper and set a heavy book on top for several days. When they're flat and dry, set them on the front of a folded card. Cover them with clear adhesive paper.